"Why are penguins black and white?"

... and other

Questions Kids Ask™

About Birds, Reptiles & Amphibians

SCHOLASTIC

**New York   Toronto   London   Auckland   Sydney
Mexico City   New Delhi   Hong Kong   Buenos Aires**

QUESTIONS KIDS ASK ABOUT BIRDS, REPTILES & AMPHIBIANS

Dear QKA Reader,

Reptiles are just about the coolest creatures on Earth! I know because I happen to be one. Oh sure, some people think we're creepy and cold-blooded, but they just don't know us. That's why I'm so excited that you're reading this book. It will teach you about my family and me. You'll meet my relatives, the skinks. (They're lots of fun at family reunions.) Plus you'll learn about some of my distant cousins: snakes and frogs.

Are you wondering why they let birds into this book? Me, too. (Especially since some birds eat lizards!) It turns out that birds might have been related to us reptiles millions of years ago. That's what some herpetologists and ornithologists believe. You'll find more about this at the end of the book. And if you're not sure who herpetologists and ornithologists are, don't worry. There's information about them inside, too.

So, read on! And keep on asking questions.

Your pondering pal,

Leonardo da Lizard

P.S. I can blend into a book about reptiles and their relatives pretty easily, but if you're sharp you'll spot me on every page!

Crows and other common birds don't usually fly above 300 feet (91 m). But some birds can soar much higher. Migrating whooper swans, for instance, can fly higher than 27,000 feet (8,230 m)—more than 178 times the height of the Statue of Liberty! But the trophy for the highest flyer goes to the Ruppell's griffon, a type of vulture. In 1973, a Ruppell's griffon collided with an airplane at 37,000 feet (11,278 m). At that height, a human would die because of a lack of oxygen. A griffon can live on very little oxygen because of its light weight and rapid heartbeat.

In general, most birds fly at high altitudes when they migrate. Because they need to conserve their strength, migrating birds seek rising air currents, called thermals, to help them glide and soar. Flying in a V-shaped formation also helps the birds fly higher and longer because they use less energy flying this way.

How high can birds fly?

The sky's the limit for our fine-feathered friends!

Canceled Flight

EXTRA

The heaviest bird that can fly is the great bustard. It can weigh up to 46 pounds (20.9 kg)—that's as much as an average six-year-old kid!

The ostrich, the world's largest bird, can run up to 45 miles per hour (72 kph), but it can't fly.

The tiny hummingbird, a beautiful solo traveler, is the only bird that can fly in reverse. Special qualities allow it to perform this feat and many others.

The hummingbird can flap its wings faster than any other bird—up to 200 times per second. Its wings and shoulder joints are specially shaped. In proportion to its body size, its flight muscles are the largest of all birds.

All these features allow the hummingbird to fly forward, backward, sideways, up, down, and upside down. It can even hover like a miniature helicopter—a move that uses 10 times the energy of a marathon runner! To get the energy they need, hummingbirds eat food that weighs about half their own weight every day.

Can birds fly backward?

One particular bird can, and does.

EXTRA

The rapid flapping of a hummingbird's wings creates the soft humming sound that gives the bird its name.

Feed Me!

Hummingbirds prefer flowers with red blossoms and lots of nectar. Here are some of their favorites:

Coral bells   Impatiens
Gladiolus   Bleeding heart   Hibiscus

How many feathers does a bird have?

It depends on what kind of bird it is.

Feather Facts

Swans have the most feathers: 20,000–25,000
Hummingbirds have the fewest feathers: 900–1,000

The number of feathers a bird has depends mainly on where it lives and what it does. Songbirds typically have 2,000 to 4,000 feathers, with as many as 1,000 on their heads. Some swans have as many as 25,000 feathers, with 20,000 of them on their heads!

Ostriches, which live in warm climates, have no feathers on their heads. This keeps them cool in the sun. Scavenger birds, such as vultures, have few feathers on their heads because feathers would get in the way as they feed on their messy prey. Birds that live in cool climates have the most feathers on their heads. Scientists believe the feathers protect their brains from severe temperature changes.

A bird's feathers make up almost $\frac{1}{5}$ of its body weight. Feathers give a bird's wings a shape that makes it possible to fly. Feathers also help keep the bird clean and dry, and they protect it from the cold.

Do birds shed their feathers?

Yes, but it doesn't happen all at once.

Average Molting Time:

BIRD	MOLTING TIME
Penguins	Two weeks
Robins	One month
Peacocks	Seven months for their tails

Birds are the only animals in the world that are covered in feathers. Every year, birds lose their feathers and grow new ones at least once and as many as three times. This process is called molting.

Most birds molt in the late summer or early fall. Usually, the feathers fall off at different times. This way, no part of the bird is bare at any time. Wing and tail feathers often molt in such a way that birds can still fly. During the breeding season, many mother birds lose feathers on their lower chest. This way, the heat from their body is closer to their eggs and keeps their eggs warm.

The molting season lasts between a few weeks and two months for most birds. During this time, new feathers grow.

Feathers, like human hair, aren't made of living tissue. If they become damaged, they don't heal. Damaged feathers must be replaced by new ones.

11

A bird's bill, or beak, grows continuously, just like your fingernails. In fact, your fingernails and a bird's bill are made up of the same substance: a protein called keratin. Over time, the keratin forms the hard, horny covering, or sheath, around a bird's upper and lower jaws. Keratin is also found in a bird's feathers and in your hair.

Birds don't have true teeth (though some have a jagged surface on the inside of their bills to help them hold food). Instead of chewing, birds use their bills to tear and crush food into pieces small enough to swallow.

Birds aren't the only creatures with bills. All turtles have bills, and so do some fish and at least one mammal: the duck-billed platypus. Fossils show that some dinosaurs had bills, too.

Does a bird's bill grow?

It never stops growing.

EXTRA
A bird's bill has many purposes, including gathering food, grooming, defense, climbing, playing, nest-building, and feeding itself and its babies.

Budding Beaks

Common Pet Birds' Upper Beak Rate of Growth per Year

Canary	1⅓ to 1½ inches (3.4–3.8 cm)
Parakeet	3 inches (7.62 cm)
Parrot	¼ inch (.64 cm)

Blue, red, orange, yellow, black . . . the toucan's bill may be one, two, or even all of these colors. It's much too big and colorful to overlook.

Typically, a toucan grows to about 25 inches (62.5 cm) tall. Its bill can be as much as 7½ inches (18.75 cm) long, which is about one-third of its body length! Yet even though the toucan's bill is big, it's extremely light. Inside the bill is a honeycomb of bony material with lots of air pockets.

By using its long bill, the toucan can reach tender fruit on small branches that couldn't hold its body weight. The bird plucks a fruit with the tip of its bill, then tosses the morsel into the air and opens wide to catch and swallow it. Some toucans even toss food to each other, especially when they're trying to impress a possible mate. They've also been known to "fence" with their bills—either in fun or in competition.

What bird is known for its multi-colored bill?
Hint: It's a rainforest beauty.

Toucan Territory

Toucans are native to the rainforests of Central and South America. Although toucans mainly eat fruit, they will also eat insects, small snakes, and other birds.

How do birds know when to fly south?

A change in season gives them the reason.

CALENDAR

18

EXTRA

Some birds really go the distance. The tiny ruby-throated hummingbird flies thousands of miles from Canada all the way south to Central America for the winter.

There's a chill in the air. The days are shorter, and there's a lot less action in the backyard bird feeder. Why? It's a seasonal thing. The position of the Sun low in the sky, the fewer hours of daylight, and the shrinking supply of seeds and berries are all clues to birds that it may be time to head for warmer weather. In other words—it's time to fly south for the winter. Migrating birds know instinctively that in order to survive they have to move to where food and warmth are more plentiful.

When spring comes and days are longer, chemicals trigger the birds' urge to reproduce. They usually want to nest in the place where they grew up. So they head back north to their old nesting grounds, lay their eggs, and start the whole cycle over again.

Why don't birds fall off branches when they sleep?

Their feet don't lose their grip.

Not all birds sleep in trees, but most songbirds do. Songbirds, also called perching birds or passerines, can perch on thin branches or even telephone wires. They sleep standing up without falling off or tipping over.

The secret is in a special tendon. Tendons are like strings or cords that connect muscles to bones. Songbirds have a long tendon in each leg that stretches from thigh to toe, going through both the knee and the ankle. As a bird sits, its weight causes the tendon to stretch. As the knee bends, the bird's toes flex out and curl around the branch. In effect, the toes "lock" onto the branch. To let go, the bird relaxes its toes.

Other tendons under the toe bones prevent a bird from flipping over and hanging upside down while still holding onto the branch. The bird's grasp is so strong that it can remain perched even when the wind blows.

15

Flamingos live in warm places where there are plenty of saltwater lakes and lagoons. Liking things wet and relatively quiet, flamingos will move to another nesting area if the water runs dry or there's too much activity around their current home.

These long-legged birds spend most of their day with their heads in the water, eating tiny shrimp, algae, and crayfish—their favorite foods. It's this food that gives flamingos their pink color.

On their natural diet, flamingos would always be a healthy pink. But when they're kept in zoos, flamingos are fed nutrient-rich animal chow. It's good for their health, but their color fades. So most zookeepers add to, or supplement, the birds' diet with carrot juice or a natural vegetable dye to help keep their rosy hue.

Why are flamingos pink?

Their rosy hue comes from their food.

Food Filter

The inside of a flamingo's bill is like a built-in strainer. When the flamingo takes a mouthful of water, its tongue moves back and forth really fast. This action separates the water from the food. The flamingo then spits out the water and swallows the food. Some ducks feed in a similar way.

They may look like they're dressed for a formal dinner party, but penguins' feather "tuxedos" are actually perfect disguises. Penguins' coloring—white fronts and black or blue-gray backs—is nature's way of protecting the birds from their enemies.

Called protective coloration, this special coloring hides penguins while they are swimming. From above, their dark back feathers blend in with the deep, dark-colored, ocean water. When predators swim below penguins, their pale belly feathers help the birds blend in with the lighter-colored water along the ocean's surface.

Feathers trap air next to penguins' skin. The penguins' body heat warms the air. This keeps the penguins warm and toasty. So even though penguins may look over-dressed, they're actually perfectly outfitted for life.

Why are penguins black and white?

They're hiding in plain sight.

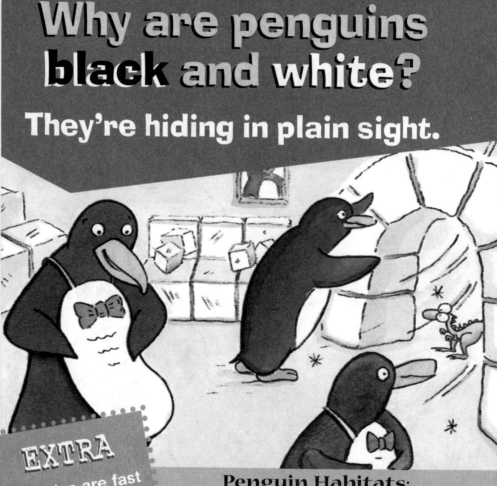

EXTRA

Penguins are fast swimmers. Some species can reach speeds of up to 30 miles per hour (48 kph).

Penguin Habitats:

Antarctic	New Zealand
South Africa	South America
Australia	Galápagos Islands

Why can't some birds fly?

Some birds don't need to.

EXTRA

Flightless birds still face danger, so they have various methods to escape. Ostriches can usually outrun their enemies. Penguins swim away from trouble. Kiwis hide in hollow logs or burrows. And long-legged cassowaries have been known to give a swift kick to animals or humans who annoy them.

The world's biggest birds are simply too heavy to get off the ground. They include Australia's ostrich, emu, and cassowary, as well as South America's rhea.

Yet not all flightless birds are huge. Flightless penguins grow to be 4 feet (1.2 m) tall at most. The flightless kiwi bird is about the size of a chicken.

So why are these birds different? Scientists believe they don't fly because they don't have to. Most birds use flight to escape from predators. Flightless birds live in places where they don't have as many predators to escape from. That's why you'll find flightless birds mainly in remote regions or on islands where animals and plants have developed, or evolved, to suit their surroundings.

What's the biggest bird?

It could look down at a professional basketball player.

Ostriches can grow to be 8 feet (7.3 m) tall and weigh as much as 300 pounds (136 kg). They're mighty big birds! In fact, ostriches are the largest birds alive today.

Ostriches can't fly. They're just too heavy to get off the ground. But they can run really fast—up to 43 miles per hour (69.2 kph)—which is how they escape their enemies. And it seems to work! Ostriches live to be about 70 years old, longer than most other earth-bound animals except for humans. Ostriches' long life expectancy is also due to the fact that they have relatively few enemies in their grasslands habitat.

Ostriches' legs are built for running. They're long and bare, with strong thighs and only two toes on each foot—fewer than any other bird.

EXTRA

Ostriches eat plants that require a very long intestine to digest. The intestine of an ostrich measures 46 feet (14 m) long. That's about one and a half times as long as the average human's!

19

Why do peacocks spread their feathers?

Their bright colors are meant to get attention.

Most male birds try to attract mates by using signals. Some inflate their pouches; others do a special dance. But the male peacock puts on one of the most spectacular displays in all of nature to impress a female.

A peacock has a long train of feathers that drags behind his body. These feathers aren't part of his tail, but grow out of his back. The peacock will wait for a female, called a peahen, to cross his path. When she does, the male spreads his 200 shiny-colored, or iridescent, feathers in the shape of an upright fan. He'll strut slowly in front of the female, moving his wings up and down, hoping she'll be wowed by his beauty. If the female likes what she sees, she just may join him as his mate.

20

Beautiful Variety

The most commonly known peacocks are from India. In fact, they're the national bird of that country. They have shiny green-blue necks and chests, with a slightly more purplish body. Their feathers are green with bright spots that resemble eyes. Other types of peacocks have feathers that are gray, bluish, or striped.

Owls have sharp hearing because of the way their ears are constructed. Hidden beneath feathers, flaps of skin form the owl's "outer ears." Beneath the ear flaps, the owl's ears have two different shapes and are positioned on either side of its head at varying heights.

This means that an owl hears sounds differently in each ear. By turning its head, the owl "equalizes" the sound until it's the same in both ears. This helps the bird pinpoint precisely where the sound is coming from, even in total darkness.

An owl hunts at night. By listening carefully it can hear the rustle of small animals hidden in the dark underbrush. Then, quickly and silently, the owl swoops in and captures animals to eat.

Do owls have keen hearing?

You bet! Even their feathers help them hear better.

EXTRA
A ring of feathers around each owl eye and fluffy feathers covering the owl's beak direct sound toward its ears.

Night Vision

Owls have excellent night vision. Their eyes are so sensitive to light during the day that they remain half-closed.

Loons really are sensible birds. They live on or near lakes in the northern United States and Canada, building nests on shore. They're excellent swimmers and divers. To chase the fish and shellfish they like to eat, loons commonly dive 6.5 to 13 feet (2–4 m) underwater. They've been known to go as deep as 100 feet (30 m) or more. Because loons hunt by sight, they survive best where the water is clean and clear.

So where did the expression "crazy as a loon" come from? It actually comes from the loon's weird call. When loons are excited, they make noises that sound like crazy laughter. If they're really upset, loons will "run" across the water, flapping their wings and cackling. To people who don't know better, this looks like loons are a bit nutty. In truth, they're just defending themselves and their young from danger.

Are loons crazy?
It's their call that's "loony."

Can roadrunners fly?

Yes, but they prefer ground transportation.

EXTRA

Roadrunners build nests 3 to 15 feet (.9–4.6 m) above the ground, hidden in underbrush or among cactuses or small trees.

Roadrunners can fly if they want to. And they sometimes do—if they need to make a fast getaway from extreme danger. Otherwise, roadrunners prefer to travel by foot.

These speedy birds can be seen running around the deserts and dry plains of the American southwest and Central America. When they're really moving, they can run as fast as 15 miles per hour (24 kph).

Roadrunners are related to cuckoos, though roadrunners' calls are much gentler. When roadrunners use their voices, it can sound like a wooden clatter or a coo. To roadrunners looking for mates, their coos are like saying, "I love you!" to other roadrunners. Male roadrunners have also been known to try to win the favor of females by bringing them plump lizards to eat!

Sometimes roadrunners eat small mammals and birds. But they usually feed on lizards, snakes, insects, spiders, scorpions, and snakes.

23

Why do birds sing?

It's their way of communicating.

Sounds Like

Some birds get their names from the sounds they make. The whippoorwill says "whip-poor-will." The gray catbird mews like a cat. And a hummingbird makes a humming sound when it flaps its wings really fast.

Cheerily, cheery-me! An American robin sings this familiar song in early spring. He's probably looking for a mate, or he might be warning other robins that this is his territory. Just as if they were putting up "Stay Away!" signs near their nests, many birds sing songs to let other birds know, "This place is taken."

In most bird species, the males do all the singing. One exception is the northern cardinal; the female sings, too.

Basically, birds make two types of sounds—calls and songs. Calls are short, simple tunes with only two or three notes. These sounds give information, such as "There's food over here" or "I'm in trouble." Songs last longer and have many different notes that follow a pattern. Other birds can tell the species, gender, and age of the singer by the song. This is especially helpful during mating season.

Can parrots talk?

They're the birds with the words.

Early Pets

Parrots were among the first animals tamed by humans. The Romans kept parrots as pets as early as 200 B.C.

Yes, some parrots can talk, but nobody really knows how parrots learn to do it. They don't have vocal cords, and their tongues are thick and clumsy. But many do learn how to copy human sounds with amazing accuracy. Some researchers think parrots use their throat muscles to create the sounds they make.

Not all species of parrots can talk, and some, like the popular African gray, don't talk until they're over a year old. Some people play tapes for their parrots, but experts say they learn best by being around and listening to people.

Do parrots understand what they're saying? Sometimes. Often, parrots just repeat what they hear, but they can be taught to request a particular food or to ask to have their necks scratched. In addition to words, they can also learn to copy, or mimic music, other birds, and even the beep of a cellular phone. So, be careful of what your parrot hears!

25

Nenes are also known as Hawaiian geese, and they live in the Aloha State. They're Hawaii's official state bird, but until recently, you would have had a hard time finding them in the wild. In 1950, there were only about 30 nenes left on Earth—the species had almost been wiped out. Zoologists and ornithologists, scientists who study birds, have worked hard to breed nenes in captivity.

By the 1960s, some zoo-bred nenes were reintroduced to the wild. Today, there are about 3,000 nenes. The species is still endangered, but with continued hard work, nenes will survive.

Nenes nest in hollows along the slopes of volcanoes. They line their hollows with dried grass and other soft materials to make the nests cozy. Unlike most geese, nenes don't migrate. They live in Hawaii all year long. (If you lived in the beautiful islands of Hawaii, you wouldn't want to leave either!)

Where do nenes live?
They nest on the slopes of volcanoes.

Pet Problem

Nenes survived well in Hawaii until humans introduced such animals as dogs and cats to the islands. The birds have no defenses against these predators.

There's nothing a snail kite likes better than soaring over the Florida Everglades hunting for apple snails. When it spots one, the snail kite swoops down from the sky and grabs the snail in its sharp claws.

Then the bird finds a quiet place to eat. Standing on one foot, while holding the snail in the other, the snail kite uses its sharp curved beak to pick the snail from its shell. Gulp!

Like all the birds in the kite family, snail kites are hawks. Yet, unlike most hawks, snail kites are picky eaters. Most hawks vary their diets—a lizard here, a mouse there—but snail kites will eat only apple snails. If apple snails disappear, so will snail kites.

The apple snails' habitat of clean, shallow fresh water is shrinking mainly because of development and water pollution. So, the snail kite's habitat is shrinking, too. The snail kite is now an endangered species.

EXTRA

The snail kite is not a superfast flyer. There's no need for speed to catch a slow-moving snail.

What is the snail kite's favorite food?

Hint: It doesn't eat kites!

What does an ornithologist do?

This scientist studies things with wings.

Help Wanted

Ornithologists may work for museums or zoos. Some of them work at colleges and universities, where they teach students how to study birds. Others work for fish and wildlife organizations helping to save endangered birds and their habitats.

Ornithologists are scientists who study birds. The name comes from the Greek word *ornis*, which means "bird."

Most ornithologists study a particular type of birds or one part of bird life. For instance, some ornithologists focus on birdcalls and songs. They want to know how birds communicate with each other. Which sounds are meant to alert other birds to danger? Which sounds are meant to attract a mate? An ornithologist might spend months recording wild bird songs and then listening to them in the laboratory to find the answers.

Other ornithologists study how birds fly, how they choose mates, or how they build nests. Humans have a lot to learn about birds. No wonder some scientists devote their lives to studying our feathered friends!

What does a herpetologist do?

Snakes and salamanders are a specialty.

DR. AL I. GATOR

Animal Study

Herpetology is the study of reptiles and amphibians. Here are other zoology (animal study) specialties:

Ornithology - Study of Birds

Ichthyology - Study of Fish

Mammalogy - Study of Mammals

Entomology - Study of Insects

Herpetologists are the zoologists who study reptiles and amphibians. Herpetologists who are most interested in reptile and amphibian behavior do much of their research in the animal's natural habitat. Out in the field, they watch animals hunt, hide from predators, mate, and care for their young. Other herpetologists study the way reptile and amphibian bodies work. These scientists do much of their research in laboratories, where they can perform experiments to find out how and why animals do what they do.

To become a professional herpetologist, you'd need to study biology, chemistry, physics, and math, as well as computer science and statistics. As a herpetologist, you might find yourself analyzing such things as a lizard's lunch or a turtle's toenails. To do this you have to be very organized and patient.

29

Snakes don't have ears, so they don't hear sounds at all. They can't see very well, either. Snakes are such good hunters because their other senses make up for what's missing.

Snakes are sensitive to vibrations, or movement, around them. They also have an excellent sense of smell and can follow a scent trail by using their tongue, much like we use our noses.

The tip of a snake's forked tongue carries the scent back into a pair of holes in the top of the snake's mouth. These holes connect directly to the snake's brain, allowing it to sense that some prey is nearby.

Snakes also locate their prey by sensing the heat given off by the prey's body. Tiny pits, on either side of snakes' heads, sense the heat given off by the bodies of other animals. Snakes then move their heads until the heat signal is centered between the two pits. Then they strike.

30

Can snakes hear?
No, but they make up for it in other ways.

How do snakes move without feet?

They're successful slitherers.

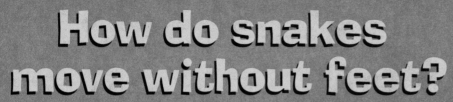

EXTRA

To climb a tree, most snakes wrap their tails firmly around the tree trunk, then stretch their front part farther up, wrapping it around a branch. Then they pull up their tail ends, inching up in an accordian-like way.

Depending on their weight, length, and environment, snakes move their bodies differently to slither along the ground or up trees. They use their strong muscles, flexible backbone, and special belly scales, called scutes, to move.

Lightweight snakes twist their bodies into a series of wavy S-curves, pushing backward and outward against rough places on the ground to slither forward on their scutes. Heavier snakes travel in a straight line. While one set of scutes holds part of their body in place, another set ripples forward and digs into the ground. Then that set holds on, and another set inches forward.

Other types of snakes move sideways. They press their rear part down, make a loop of their forepart, and sling it sideways, especially when the ground is hot. Then they loop and throw their rear into position and repeat the process, without ever letting their midsection touch the ground.

31

When most animals, including humans, encounter a rattlesnake, they have a good reason to be afraid. Rattlers can be deadly.

King snakes, though, have a different attitude. They're not frightened of rattlesnakes at all. Because king snakes have a natural immunity to most types of snake venom, they're fearless around other snakes. In fact, king snakes have been known to feed on other snakes, as well as rodents, lizards, and birds. Although they kill their prey by coiling around it and suffocating it, king snakes pose no threat to humans.

Sleek, striped king snakes live in the Midwest and Southwest United States. They prefer to live in forests. And while they live mainly on the ground, they've also been known to climb trees. They usually hunt for food in the morning and at dusk.

What's unusual about king snakes?

A rattlesnake bite causes no fright.

Rattlesnake Fear

King snakes usually grow to be 3 to 6.5 feet (1–2 m) long. Rattlesnakes can be bigger than king snakes, but they're still afraid of king snakes. If they see or smell one, rattlesnakes will slither away and hide.

Anacondas love the water and are good swimmers. They can swim underwater for surprisingly long periods. That's why they're sometimes called water boas. They live in warm, wet regions of South America.

Anacondas can grow to be 30 feet (9 m) long and are one of the heaviest snakes on Earth. They stalk their prey and kill it by drowning it or squeezing it until it dies from lack of air. Then anacondas swallow the animal whole. And, they're not afraid to go after big targets! Anacondas have been known to eat deer and even crocodiles.

Unlike some snakes that lay eggs, anacondas give birth to live young. Female anacondas usually give birth to 40 or 50 babies, but they may have as many as 100 at one time! Baby anacondas are between 2 and 3 feet (.6 and 1 m) long when they're born.

What type of environment do anacondas like?

They prefer the tropics.

Blending In

Anacondas are greenish-gray with black spots. Their coloring helps them blend in with the mud and grass on the riverbanks where they live.

Why do turtles have shells?

It's a matter of security.

ED'S SHELL SALES

NICE!

NEW!

USED!

TODAY'S SPECIAL

A turtle's shell offers protection. This slow-moving, toothless animal can tuck its head, legs, and tail into its shell to hide when an enemy is near. The shell also protects many of the turtle's organs, including its heart. A turtle shell is separated into two sections: one piece on the turtle's back and another on its chest.

Most turtle shells are made up of many flat bony shields. Over these lie broad, thin layers of keratin, a tough material that also makes up your fingernails. These colored layers may be brown, black, or olive green with various dots and markings, depending on the kind of turtle.

Some turtles, such as softshell turtles, have a leathery skin covering instead of layers of keratin. These turtles rely on their sharp claws and jaws for defense.

EXTRA

Many of the turtles that live in water hibernate underwater during winter. They bury themselves in the muck found at the bottom of the body of water and breathe by absorbing oxygen from the water.

Turtle Tacklers

Some animals that prey on turtles:

Bears	Birds
Crocodiles	Otters
Raccoons	Snakes

How long can a giant tortoise live?

Left alone, they live a long, long life.

Tortoise Talk

Giant tortoises have existed since prehistoric times. Because they live on remote islands with few predators, they have been able to grow so large and live such long lives.

Giant tortoises, which live on the Galápagos Islands west of South America and on the Seychelles Islands in the Indian Ocean, can live more than 100 years. Many reach 150 years—if humans leave them alone.

Historically, sailors and explorers hunted the giant reptiles for their meat. People still hunt them today, which is why most of the world's giant tortoises are relatively young. Their older, bigger relatives were killed by hunters. The Aldabra tortoise once occupied several islands in the Indian Ocean. Today, only about 150,000 Aldabra tortoises remain in the Seychelles.

Healthy giant tortoises can grow to be more than 4 feet (1.2 m) long and weigh 400 to 500 pounds (181–227 kg). They graze on grass and shrubs and spend a lot of time simply resting in the Sun.

35

If you've ever touched a frog or a toad, you've already put your finger on one big difference: their skin. Frogs have skin that is smooth and moist. Toads have dry, rough skin, which is often covered with bumpy warts.

Frogs are better jumpers than toads. Most frogs have teeth; toads do not. However, frogs and toads are alike in a very important way: They're both amphibians—they live part of their lives in the water and part on land.

When they're babies, or tadpoles, frogs and toads stay underwater. They breathe through gills as fish do. But as the tadpoles grow up, they lose their gills and develop lungs so that they can breathe air.

Adult frogs stay close to the water. But you'll find toads on land—often hopping around sunny places.

What's the difference between frogs and toads?

Plenty—and it's more than skin deep.

At first glance, it's hard to see any difference between alligators and crocodiles. But a closer look reveals that alligators have broader snouts than crocodiles. Alligators will only live in freshwater, and sometimes slightly salty water. Most crocodiles live in freshwater, too, but one species actually lives in the ocean.

Teeth are another giveaway. Crocodiles have a tooth on each side of the bottom jaw that stays over their "lips" when they close their mouths. Alligators do not. Crocodiles live in the tropics, while alligators are found in colder climates.

But there are more similarities than differences. Both alligators and crocodiles are reptiles—cold-blooded meat-eating creatures—that live in and around water. Both animals hatch from eggs, which the parents guard until the young are born.

How are crocodiles and alligators different?
Their teeth tell a lot.

CONTESTANT #1

CONTESTANT #2

Tall Tales

Ever heard a story like this? A pet alligator flushed down the toilet grows up to terrorize a town? Relax! It has never happened. Stories like these are known as "urban legends."

How did dinosaurs become extinct?

Perhaps something made a huge impact.

Dinosaurs were one of the most successful groups of animals ever to live on Earth. Then, about 65 million years ago, they suddenly disappeared. For many years, scientists have argued over what caused the dinosaurs to die out. Some think massive volcanic eruptions caused their disappearance. Others think it was caused by radiation from the explosion of a very large star. The most popular theory suggests that the cause was a rock from space!

In the early 1980s, scientists Luis and Walter Alvarez examined rocks deposited at the same time dinosaurs disappeared. They discovered an element that is rare on Earth but very common in asteroids. These scientists and others think that about 65 million years ago, a huge asteroid hit Earth. The asteroid landed in Chicxulub, Mexico. They believe the impact caused so much damage that dinosaurs and thousands of other animal and plant species died.

What was the biggest dinosaur?

The most giant of the giants might still be uncovered.

Meat-eating Giants

For a long time, *Tyrannosaurus rex*—at 40 feet (12 m) long—was thought to be the biggest meat-eating dinosaur. However, in the 1990s, evidence of two larger predators was discovered in Argentina: *Giganotosaurus*—41 feet (12.3 m) long, and another dinosaur that may have been 45 feet (13.5 m) long!

The largest complete dinosaur skeleton ever found was that of the *Brachiosaurus*. This plant-eater was about 73 feet (22 m) long, 46 feet (14 m) tall, and may have weighed up to 190 tons! There may have been dinosaurs twice as large as *Brachiosaurus*. However, paleontologists (scientists who study prehistoric life) haven't found complete skeletons, so they can't determine whether these dinosaurs were truly bigger.

Proof will have to wait until complete skeletons are found. Dinosaurs in competition for the title of biggest include these plant-eaters: *Diplodocus*—may have been up to 90 feet (27 m) long, 50 feet (15 m) tall, and weighed as much as 12 tons; *Argentinosaurus*—may have been up to 130 feet (39 m) long and weighed as much as 100 tons; and *Supersaurus*—may have been up to 120 feet (36 m) long and weighed as much as 55 tons.

39

Skinks are lizards that are found almost all over the world—especially in the South Pacific, Asia, and North Africa. Some skinks like wet environments, and some like dry, but they all prefer warm, mild climates.

Most skinks live in underground burrows. They come out in the early morning or late afternoon to feed on insects, snails, spiders, and worms. Some species will eat small reptiles, too.

Skinks generally have smooth, glossy skin. Their colors vary from species to species. For instance, Berber's skinks are golden brown with orange markings. Five-lined skinks are born with bright blue tails that turn black over time. And the blue-tongued skink of Australia looks like an ordinary gray-brown lizard—until it opens its mouth, and out pops a big, blue tongue!

40

What's a skink?
It's an undercover lizard.

Green Climbing Machine

The green-blood skink is most unusual. With its sticky toe pads and strong limbs, the green-scaled skink is especially good at climbing. It also has a green tongue, lays green eggs, and yes, even has green blood!

Salamander is the common name for about 320 different kinds of amphibians, which are animals that can live in water and on land. Unlike such amphibians as frogs, salamanders have tails. Newts, axolotls, and mud puppies are just a few types of salamanders.

Salamanders live in the warm, wet regions north of the equator. To stay moist, they use their mucus-producing skin glands. Some salamanders are bright red or yellow, and many have spots or stripes. Large-eyed and short-legged, they can be as small as 4 inches (10 cm) long or as long as 70 inches (180 cm).

Salamanders are usually nocturnal, coming out at night to hunt. They mainly eat worms and insects. Many animals prey on salamanders, but thanks to the toxic liquid made by glands in their skin, salamanders leave a bad taste in the mouth of any animal that tries to eat them!

What's a salamander?

It's a slippery character.

EXTRA

Female salamanders produce hundreds of eggs at once. Three to five years can pass between the time an egg is fertilized and the time when it turns into a young salamander.

41

Some scientists believe there once was an animal that was part-bird and part-reptile. They call this creature *Archaeopteryx*, and it lived about 150 million years ago. *Archaeopteryx* fossils were discovered more than 100 years ago.

Archaeopteryx looked like a dinosaur with wings. It had feathers like a bird's and teeth like a reptile's. It could fly like a bird, but it also had a long tail like a lizard's. It had feet like a bird's, and a snout like a reptile's. What a confusing combination!

Is it possible that *Archaeopteryx* was the first—and last—animal to combine bird and reptile features? Scientists are still trying to figure out if *Archaeopteryx* is the "missing link" between reptiles and birds.

Are birds and reptiles related?

They are linked by a fantastic fossil.

EXTRA
Before *Archaeopteryx*, scientists assumed that all dinosaurs were reptiles. Now they aren't so sure.

— QUESTIONS KIDS ASK ABOUT BIRDS, REPTILES & AMPHIBIANS —

captivity [KAP-ti-vuh-tee] for animals, the state of being raised in a zoo or other protected area

endangered species [in-DAYN-juhrd SPEE-sheez] animals that are in danger of dying out, or becoming extinct

evolve [e-VOLV] to change or adapt

habitat [HA-buh-tat] the place where an animal or plant normally lives and grows

hibernate [HEYE-buhr-nayt] to pass a period of time in a resting state in order to survive difficult conditions, such as an extremely cold winter

immunity [I-MYOO-nuh-tee] a natural resistance to or protection against something, such as the venom from snakes

inhabit [in-HA-buht] to live in

intestine [in-TES-tuhn] the part of an animal's digestive system in which most food is changed, or broken down, into simpler forms and used by the body

iridescent [ir-uh-DE-suhnt] when colors change and produce a shiny rainbow effect

keratin [KER-uh-tin] the tough material that makes up bird beaks, turtle shells, horns, hoofs, hair, fingernails, and toenails

migrate [MEYE-grayt], migrating [MEYE-grayt-ing] to move from one place to another

migratory [MEYE-gruh-tor-ee] having to do with moving from one place to another

mimic [MI-mik] to imitate or copy something carefully

molting [MOHL-ting] when birds shed their feathers and other animals shed their fur or skin

nocturnal [nok-TUHR-nuhl] animals that are busy, or active, during the night

ornithologist [or-nuh-THO-luh-jist] a scientist who studies birds

passerines [PA-suh-reyenz] the largest order of birds, which includes more than half of all living birds, consisting mostly of perching songbirds

paleontologist [pay-lee-on-TO-luh-jist] a scientist who studies prehistoric life

predator [PRE-duh-tuhr] an animal that hunts other animals

protective coloration [pruh-TEK-tiv kuh-luh-RAY-shuhn] the special coloring of some animals' fur or feathers that helps them to blend in with their surroundiings

scutes [skootz] the bony or horny covering or special scales on some animals, such as the belly scales on snakes

species [SPEE-sheez] a group of animals or plants that are alike in certain ways

QUESTIONS KIDS ASK ABOUT BIRDS, REPTILES & AMPHIBIANS

supplement [SUH-pluh-ment] to add to

tendon [TEN-duhn] the tissue in animals' bodies that connects muscles to bones

territory [TER-uh-tohr-ee] a place that is occupied and defended by an animal or group of animals

thermal [THER-muhl] a rising body of warm air

venom [VE-nuhm] poison made by some animals, such as snakes

zoologist [zoo-O-luh-jist] a scientist who studies animals

QUESTIONS KIDS ASK ABOUT BIRDS, REPTILES & AMPHIBIANS